Introduction to Peking Opera

SHENG

By Zhou Chuanjia

Illustrated by Pangbudun'er

RC

Books Beyond Boundaries

ROYAL COLLINS

2

Xu Ce

Hua Yun

Ren Tanghui

Qin Qiong

Liu Shichang

Zhu Geliang

Zhao Yun

Wang Jinlong

Huang Zhong

Liu Xiu

Zhou Yu

4

Wu Yunzhao

Yang Bo

Fan Zhongyu

Emperor Zhengde

Gao Chong

Guan Yu

Yang Zongbao

Sun Wukong

Liang Shanbo

Huang Tianba

Mo Ji

5

Old *Sheng*

Old *Sheng* is the name for male characters with long beards. That's why they are also called the "Bearded *Sheng*." Let's take a look!

Crown

This is the headdress for emperors in the opera. There are tassels for it that can be put on or removed. Old *Sheng* characters like emperors are also called Old *Sheng* in the crown.

There are many different characters who belong in this category. Some may have a very high status. As high as the emperor, for example, Emperor Liu Xiu in *Hitting the Golden Brick*.

Yellow Dragon Robe

The dragon robes are decorated with four-toed-dragons called *mang*. Only emperors can wear yellow.

Jade Belt

Emperors and officials wear it to show their status. When they walk, they hold it with both hands.

Martial *Sheng's* Headdress

This is the cap that martial artists wear in everyday situations.

Xuezi Robe

This is the robe that male characters wear in general.

Wind Cap

This is the cap that male characters wear to show it's windy.

Emperor Zhengde in *Wandering Dragon Lusting Phoenix:*

Emperor Zhengde is on a private tour away from the palace. He doesn't want others to know who he is, so he is not wearing the yellow robe.

In ancient times, the emperor was of course the supreme figure. Below the emperor, there were many officials of different levels. Let's see what their costumes look like in Peking Opera.

Chancellor's Headdress

Xu Ce was a chancellor back in the Tang Dynasty (7th–10th century). He enjoyed a distinguished identity among all officials, so his headdress was also more glamorous than anyone else's.

Xu Ce in *Running up the Rampart Tower*

Reformed Dragon Robe

A reformed dragon robe is a simpler version of the traditional dragon robes, like the one for Yang Bo on page 9.

Black Gauze Cap

The black gauze gap with two squared wings on the sides is for loyal ministers. The Old *Sheng* characters with the gauze cap and dragon robes are also called Old *Sheng* in robe and belt.

Ivory *Hu*

The ivory *hu* is a ritual baton that ministers hold when they have an audience with the emperor in court. They will write down what they want to report on the *hu* as a reminder for themselves, so the *hu* is like a special "notebook" for important officials.

Green Dragon Robe

This is also called the green coiling dragon robe because the embroidered dragons on the robe coil up in circles. This robe can be worn by emperors, princes, and very high-ranking officials.

Yang Bo in *Requesting a Second Audience*

One famous Old *Sheng* character is Zhuge Liang. His costume is very special – the *Bagua* Robe, or the Eight Trigrams Robe. Generally, Zhuge Liang is considered an Old *Sheng* with robe and belt as well.

The *Bagua* (Eight Trigrams) Headscarf

This is usually worn by celestial figures, Daoist practitioners, and military strategists like Zhuge Liang himself.

The *Bagua* (Eight Trigrams) Robe

This is also for celestial figures, Daoist practitioners, and military strategists. The *Bagua* Headscarf goes with the *Bagua* Robe.

Feather Fan

The feather fan is a special prop for Zhuge Liang. He always carries it with him because he is so intelligent that he never panics over any unexpected situation.

Zhuge Liang in *The Talents' Gathering*

Liu Shichang in *Story of the Black Pot*

Royal Blue *Xuezi* Robe

This is usually worn by rich people or officials in everyday situations.

High Square Headscarf

This is an undecorated soft cap in a square shape; usually there is no ribbon attached. Characters who wear this headscarf can be gentlemen or regular people.

Horsewhip

When the audience sees an actor carrying a horsewhip on stage, they will know that his character is riding a horse in the play. If the actor waves the whip, that means the horse is running fast.

Black *Xuezi* Robe

The black *xuezi* robe, also called the plain black *xuezi* robe, like the one that Fan Zhongyu wears on the right, is for the poor. Characters in the *xuezi* robes like Liu Shichang and Fan Zhongyu are generally called Old *Sheng* in *xuezi*.

Fan Zhongyu in *Feast for the New Champion Scholar*

11

The characters we've seen so far, like Zhuge Liang, Liu Shichang, and Fan Zhongyu, are all scholars who do not perform martial arts. We call them Civil Old *Sheng*. Now, let's meet some characters who know how to fight, or what we call Martial Old *Sheng*.

Bound Headdress

This is the headdress for martial artists.

Huang Zhong in *Mount Dingjun*

Apricot *Kao* Armor

Kao armor is what military officers wear in battle. The armor comes in different colors. The apricot ones are usually for veterans.

Lotus Leaf Helmet

This is for military officers.

Kao Armor Flags

These flags are bound to the military officers' backs to protect them from enemies from behind. The color of the flags is the same as the *kao* armor the actor is wearing. Hua Yun in red armor will have red flags, and Huang Zhong in apricot armor will have apricot flags.

Red *Kao* Armor

We call Martial Old *Sheng* wearing the *kao* armor Old *Sheng* with the kao.

Hua Yun in *The Battle of Taiping*

13

Some Martial Old *Sheng* can fight in wars without *kao* armor. These characters are called Old *Sheng* in the archery cloak.

Archery Cloak

Both Wu Yunzhao and Qin Qiong wear archery cloaks. Qin wears black while Wu wears white.

Frontal Decoration

The frontal decoration is round with white pearls; there is also a big pom-pom attached on top. When the military officer wears it alone, it means he is defeated in the battle.

Filial Headband

This is a piece of white silk. When Wu Yunzhao's father was sentenced to death by the emperor, he wore it to show filial piety to his father.

Equestrian Jacket

Wu Yunzhao wears an equestrian jacket outside his archery cloak. These two costumes are usually worn together by Martial Old *Sheng*.

Wu Yunzhao in *Nanyang Pass*

Black *Xuezi* Robe

Unlike Wu Yunzhao, Qin Qiong wears a black *xuezi* robe outside his archery cloak. But he wears it in a distinctive style: instead of wearing it fully, he is only draped in it.

Qin Qiong in *Preparing for Battle*

Arrowhead Leaf

This is also called "hero's tip." The characters who wear it are usually heroic outlaws.

Silk Cap

Heroic figures, warriors, military commanders, and policemen can wear this kind of cap.

Golden Sword Breaker

Qin Qiong is the master of using the sword breaker and often carries two on his back.

15

Empty Fort Strategy

The Wei military officer Sima Yi and his 150 thousand troops have besieged Xicheng, where Zhuge Liang was. But Zhuge Liang's Shu army in Xicheng was deployed elsewhere, and there was no way he could fight against Sima Yi at this point. So, Zhuge Liang came up with a plan. He left the city gate wide open and sat relaxed on the rampart tower while playing his *qin* zither. When Sima Yi saw him so confident and at ease, he thought there must be an ambush in the city. He panicked and ordered his army to retreat.

"Zhuge Liang looks so calm...
Does he have all his troops
ready in the city?"

Young *Sheng*

Now we are going to meet a group of *Sheng* characters of another sub-category. They are the handsome young men, and they are called Young *Sheng*. The biggest difference between these characters and the Old *Sheng* is that they do not have beards.

Gauze Cap

A type of official cap.

Wang Jinlong in *Su San the Courtesan*

Red Dragon Robe

This is also called red coiling dragon robe.

Jade Belt

The jade belt always goes with the dragon robe or court robe. We call Young *Sheng* characters with the jade belt and gauze cap Young *Sheng* in robe and belt.

Mo Ji in *Hitting the Ungrateful Husband*

"Gilded Robe"

The poor scholar's ragged clothes have a funny name – the "gilded robe."

Poor Scholar's Headscarf

Mo Ji is very poor, and his clothes are full of holes and patches. Young *Sheng* characters like him are called poor scholars; their headscarves are called a poor scholar's headscarf.

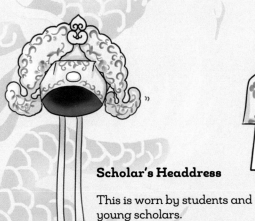

Scholar's Headdress

This is worn by students and young scholars.

Embroidered *Xuezi* Robe

The robes that Young *Sheng* characters wear are usually embroidered. This indicates they are civil and gentle.

Fan

We call Young *Sheng* characters wearing the scholar's headdress and carrying a fan, the fan scholars.

Liang Shanbo in *Story of the Willow Shade*

Three-Pointed Collar ("bitter shoulder")

Martial characters will wear this collar on their shoulders, and the collar will be in the same color as their dragon robes.

Purple Gold Crown

This headdress is also called the prince's helmet. The prince and other young military officers like Zhou Yu and Yang Zongbao can wear it. Usually, there are two tail feathers from male pheasants attached to the top of the crown, and they will greatly enrich the actors' performance. This is why we also call this type of Young *Sheng* character the *Sheng* with the feathers.

Zhou Yu in *The Talents' Gathering*

White Dragon Robe

The white robe makes Zhou Yu look very dashing.

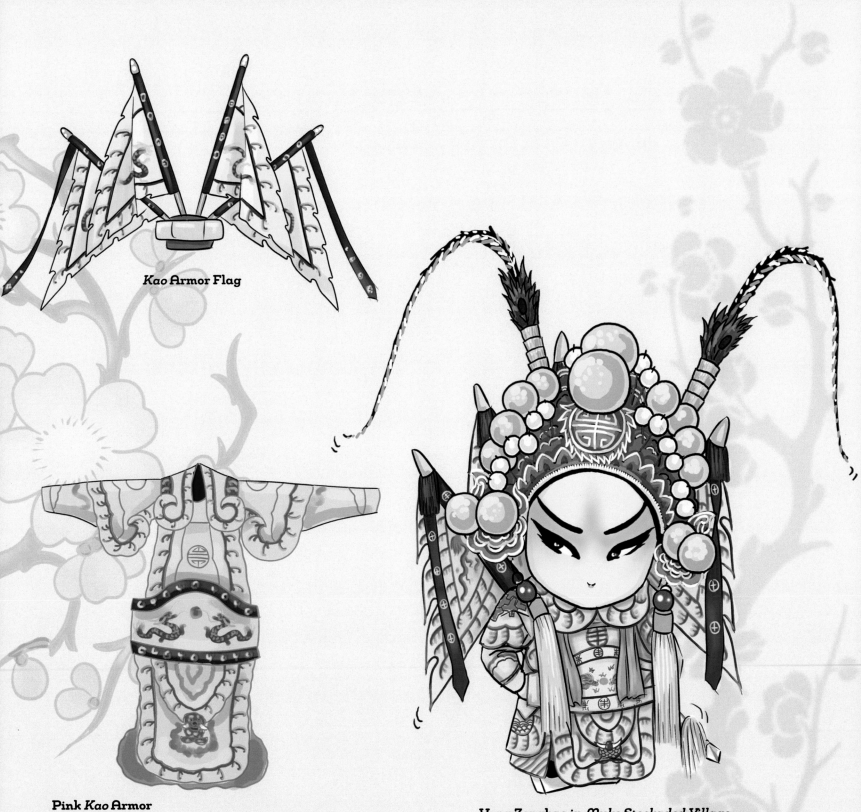

Kao Armor Flag

Pink Kao Armor

The pink armor is usually worn by young military officers. The Young *Sheng* characters who perform martial arts are called Martial Young *Sheng*.

Yang Zongbao in *Muke Stockaded Village*

21

Story of the Willow Shade

The *Story of the Willow Shade* is also called *The Butterfly Lovers.* The clever and strong-minded girl, Zhu Yingtai, wanted to go to school like the boys, so she put on boy's clothes and set off. On her way, she met a young student called Liang Shanbo, who was going to the same school as her. The two became close friends very soon, and they swore to be brothers under a willow tree.

After studying together for three years, Yingtai fell deeply in love with Shanbo. When she finished school and had to return home, Shanbo walked a long way with her to see her off. Yingtai tried to tell him about her real identity and her wish to marry him with all the metaphors she could think of, but the bookish Shanbo never took the hint.

At last, Yingtai told him that she had a little sister – her ninth sister in fact – and she wished Shanbo could come and make a marriage proposal.

Shanbo kept his promise and came to Yingtai's home. He was both surprised and happy to find out the ninth sister was none other than Yingtai herself. However, his happiness didn't last long, for he immediately heard the news that Yingtai's father had already promised to marry his daughter to another man – Ma Wencai. The heartbroken Shanbo went home and fell seriously ill. He soon died in grief.

When Yingtai learned about her lover's death, she too lost all hope to live. She made her father allow her to wear mourning clothes and visit Shanbo's grave on her wedding day. The moment Yingtai came upon the grave, a strong wind started blowing, and thunder and lightning were heard and seen in the sky. Suddenly, Shanbo's grave split open before Yingtai, who then threw herself inside without hesitation. When the storm cleared, a pair of butterflies flew out from the grave. They danced around each other as they flew away, and they would never separate again.

Martial *Sheng*

The Martial *Sheng* characters are young, powerful warriors. Some of them are military officers who fight in wars, while some are heroic outlaws who right wrongs.

Bound Helmet

Kao Armor Flag

Gao Chong in *Breaking Down the Iron War Chariot*

Green *Kao* Armor

Master Helmet

**Big Lance
(used by Gao Chong)**

**Small Lance
(used by Zhao Yun)**

***Kao* Armor Flag**

White *Kao* Armor

The armor that Zhao Yun wears is white and long. We call Martial *Sheng* wearing long armor Martial *Sheng* in Long *kao*.

Zhao Yun in *The Battle of Changban Hills*

25

Martial *Sheng* without *kao* armor is called Martial *Sheng* in short clothes.

Ren Tanghui in *Protecting the Protected*

Silk Cap

Tight Shirt

These are what warriors wear in fights.

Tight Pants

Thin Boots

Hard Silk Cap

Pom-Pom

Heroic outlaws wear it by their temples.

Martial *Sheng*'s Embroidered *Xuezi* Robe

Thick Boots

These are the boots worn by Huang Tianba as well as by all the military and civil officers mentioned earlier.

Huang Tianba in *Tianba Sweeps the Tomb*

Wait a minute, the other *Sheng* faces are all clean; why is Lord Guan's face painted so red? Is there a mistake? Great question! Although Lord Guan looks different from other *Sheng* characters we've seen so far, he is also part of the *Sheng* category. We call these red-faced *Sheng* characters, like Lord Guan and Zhao Kuangyin, Red *Sheng*. Legend says Lord Guan became a god after he died. So, people revere this character in Peking Opera as well.

Guan Yu (Lord Guan) in *The Battle of Changsha*

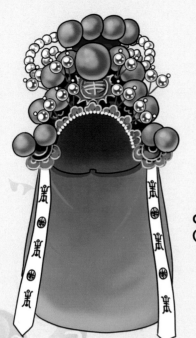

**Green Master Helmet
(just for Lord Guan)**

**Green Dragon Crescent Blade
(Lord Guan's special weapon)**

Lord Guan's *Kao* Armor

Usually, Lord Guan's armor is customized
and much more glamorous than regular
green armor. Do you see anything missing
in this picture? There are no armor flags
for Lord Guan. Those with flags are called
hard *kao*, while those without are called
soft *kao*.

Actually, many other *Sheng* characters have painted faces too. For example, our favorite Monkey King Sun Wukong is usually played by Martial *Sheng* (or Martial *Chou*) actors.

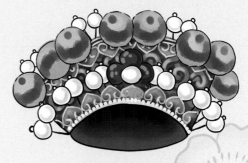

Top Helmet

**Sun Wukong in *Havoc in Heaven:
Stealing Spiritual Peaches and Elixirs***

Principle Robe (Monkey Archery Robe)

Purple Gold Crown (pheasant's tail feathers can be attached)

"Fox Tail"

The furry thing that Sun Wukong wears on his shoulders is called a "fox tail," but it is not a real fox tail of course. Usually, bandit kings and military officers of foreign troops will wear it.

Yellow Dragon Robe

Sun Wukong is the Monkey King, so he can also wear yellow.

Sun Wukong in *Havoc in Heaven: Water Curtain Cave*

31

Children's Costume

Clothes for children in the play.

Children's wig

Some of you may be wondering, are there roles for children in the *Sheng* category? Of course! In Peking Opera, these roles are known as Children *Sheng*.

Havoc in Heaven

Sun Wukong has become the Monkey King at Huaguo Mountain. The Jade Emperor in heaven worried that he might be riotous and cause trouble, so he summoned Sun Wukong to heaven and made him the imperial stableboy. When Sun Wukong understood how small and insulting his post was, he stormed out of the imperial court and returned to Huaguo Mountain. There, he appointed himself the title "The Great Sage, Heaven's Equal."

Hearing this, the Jade Emperor summoned him to heaven again and recognized his self-appointed title. But what he actually made Sun Wukong do was to guard the Queen Mother's heavenly peach garden. When the Queen's Mother later held the royal peach banquet for gods and goddesses, she excluded Sun Wukong from the guest list. This time, Sun was infuriated. He stole the heavenly peaches, the royal wine, and the immortal elixirs prepared for the celestial guests before they arrived and escaped back to his mountain. The Jade Emperor was very angry, and he sent ten thousand heavenly troops to capture Sun Wukong. But they were no match for the powerful Monkey King, who fought and defeated them all single-handed.

Let's learn more about Peking Opera (1)

Zhou Chuanjia – professor at Beijing Union University and researcher at the Central Research Institute of Culture and History.

Introduction

Peking Opera originated from Hui and Han Opera. There were nine roles in Hui Opera: *Mo; Sheng; Young Sheng; Wai; Dan; Tie; Fu* (Old *Dan*); *Jing;* and *Chou*. Han Opera had all these roles as well as an additional one called *Za*. Peking Opera reduced the roles to *Sheng, Dan, Jing, and Chou* – each containing several sub-categories.

The distinction between each role is based on their standardized characteristics and performing styles. These are defined by the characters' gender, age, identity, job, and other features. The playwright's opinions on these characters also influence how they are depicted. The audience can immediately tell who the protagonists are and who the antagonists are, right from the start of the play. Every role is unique in its singing, dialogue, performance, martial arts, costume, and makeup style. Peking Opera performance is vibrant and colorful, making it a feast for the eyes and for the ears.

The *Sheng* category

Sheng refers to male characters. It can be divided into the following sub-categories: Old *Sheng;* Young *Sheng;* Martial *Sheng;* Red *Sheng;* and Child *Sheng.*

The Old *Sheng* indicates middle-aged and elderly men in a play. Because the actors wear fake beards, this role is also called bearded *Sheng*. There are Old *Sheng* characters that features singing in their performances, especially Old *Sheng* in king's caps that interpret emperors and kings; for example, Emperor Taizong of Tang in *The Madcap Fisherman* and *Competing for Commander-in Chief*. There are Old *Sheng* characters whose performances emphasize acting, like Song Shijie in *Four Imperial Scholars*. Old *Sheng* in *kao* armor carries weapons and performs some martial arts on stage, like Huang Zhong in *Mount Dingjun*. There are also Martial Old *Sheng* and "Old *Sheng*

in archery cloaks" who performs more martial arts such as Qin Qiong in *Betrothed Brothers* and Liu Xiu in *Hitting the Golden Brick*. These actors also sing and in do *Yun* dialogues.

Young *Sheng* plays young men in a play. Those carrying a fan and wearing a *xuezi* robe are handsome young scholars. These characters do not wear fake beards. Examples are Fu Peng in *Picking up the Jade Bracelet*, and Liang Shanbo in *Story of the Willow Shade*.

The *Sheng* in gauze cap – also called the *Sheng* in robe and belt – usually features dragon robes and indicates young officials, like Wang Jinlong in *Su San the Courtesan*, and Zhao Chong in *A Family Reunion*.

Poor scholars will wear a high, square headscarf and the "gilded robe," like Wang Mingfang in *Lucky Inn*, and Mo Ji in *Hitting the Ungrateful Husband*.

The *Sheng* with pheasant's tail feathers, who wears dragon robes, *kao* armor, helmets and long feathers on top, are dukes and generals. For example, Zhou Yu in *Talents' Gathering*, and Lv Bu in *The Amazing Archer*.

Martial Young *Sheng* also indicates warriors, heroic, outlaws, and teenage heroes. They have different costumes too. Cen Peng in *Conquering Luoyang* and Yu Ziqi in *The Hegemon-King Bids His Lady Farewell* wear long armor. Li Cunxiao in Fight Over the Feast and Wang Bodang in *Nihong Pass* wear archery cloaks. An Jingsi in *Mount Feihu* and Shi Xiu in *Shi Xiu the Spy* wear short, tight outfits. Yue Yun in *The Young Warrior* as well as other child figures wear purple gold crowns or the *duzi* hairstyle.

The Young *Sheng* actors use both their natural voice and falsetto when performing. Some characters have *Yun* dialogues and *Jing-Yun* dialogues, like Gao Lishi in *The Drunken Beauty* and Chang Baotong in *Beating up the Evil Chancellor*. Some characters will do a mixed *Yun* and *Jing-Yun* dialogue, like Lu Kunjie in *Lovers in War* and Yang Zongbao in *The Battle at Hongzhou*.

Martial *Sheng* plays skilled warriors and heroic figures. Those in long armor, helmet, thick boots, and carrying long weapons are mostly commanders-in-chief and experienced fighters; for example, Gao Chong in *Breaking Down the Iron Wheel Chariot* and Zhao Yun in *Changban Hills*.

The ones in tight outfits, thin boots, silk caps, and carrying short weapons are soldiers or heroic outlaws, like Ren Tanghui in *Protecting the Protected* and Wu Song in *Shizi Hills*.

Martial *Sheng* characters in archery cloaks are between the two aforementioned sub-categories in terms of their costumes and performance, which emphasize both singing and martial arts. Examples are Shi Wengong in *Death of the Bandit Leader* and Huang Tianba in *Stealing the Imperial Horse*.

Face Painted Martial *Sheng* refers to *Sheng* characters with face paint or make-up like that of the *Jing* characters. Some plays are originally tailored for the role of Martial *Jing*, but later could be played by both the *Jing* and *Sheng*. Examples are Jiang Wei in *Mount Tielong*, Chang Yuchun in *The Champion*, and the Monkey King in *Water Curtain Cave*, *Havoc in Heaven*, and *Fire Quenching Fan*.

There is also a special sub-category called Children *Sheng*, which indicates little boys – especially in legends, like Nezha in *Chentang Pass* and *Havoc in Heaven*, Chen Xiang in *Magic Lotus Lantern*, Hong Hai'er in *Red Boy*, and Liu Hai in *Feast of Celestial Peaches*.

The Red *Sheng* refers specifically to Old *Sheng* characters with red makeup, like Lord Guan and Zhao Kuangyin. Old *Sheng*, Martial *Sheng*, and Red *Jing* can all play these characters. Red *Sheng* performances emphasize acting most, and singing is high pitched and sonorous. Jiang Wei in *General Jiang Patrols the Weary Army*, Zhao Kuangyin in *Fight Between Dragon and Tiger*, and Lord Guan in *Reunion at Gucheng* and *Battle at Fancheng* are all examples of this role, although their singing styles differ.

Before Hui Opera gained popularity in the north, plays with Lord Guan were few. Later, when actor Wang Hongshou and his troupe brought this art form to more places, more plays tailored for Lord Guan were written, such as *Reunion at Gucheng*, *Battle at Fancheng*, and *Great Warrior's Defeat at Maicheng*.

About the Author:

Zhou Chuanjia was born in 1944. He studied at Peking University and Chinese National Academy of Arts, where he received his doctorate in literature. Zhou is a professor at Beijing Union University, a researcher at the Central Research Institute of Culture and History, and an expert who enjoys the special allowance of the State Council. Zhou has been teaching and researching Chinese literature, opera history, and opera critique for a long time. His major publications include *Introduction to Opera Script Writing, Performance of Famous Dan Actors,* and *Opera: Chinese Cultural Elements.*

About the Illustrator:

Pangbudun'er is an independent writer and painter of the post-80s generation. Her work is engaging with its own unique style. She painted illustrations for *Fun Talks on the Three Kingdoms* by Cai Kangyong and Hou Wenyong; her other publications include *Raising the Curtains: Will You Hear Some Peking Opera?* and several Peking Opera picture books such as *Protecting the Protected* and *Empty Fort Strategy.*

Introduction to Peking Opera:
Sheng

By Zhou Chuanjia
Illustrated by Pangbudun'er

First published in 2022 by Royal Collins Publishing Group Inc.
Groupe Publication Royal Collins Inc.
BKM Royalcollins Publishers Private Limited

Headquarters: 550-555 boul. René-Lévesque O Montréal (Québec) H2Z1B1 Canada
India office: 805 Hemkunt House, 8th Floor, Rajendra Place, New Delhi 110 008

Original Edition © Changchun Publishing House Co., Ltd.

ISBN: 978-1-4878-0911-9

To find out more about our publications, please visit www.royalcollins.com.